THE SECRET OF THE
ABIDING
PRESENCE

THE SECRET OF THE
ABIDING
PRESENCE

Andrew Murray

PUBLICATIONS

Fort Washington, PA 19034

The Secret of the Abiding Presence

Published by CLC Publications

USA: P.O. Box 1449, Fort Washington, PA 19034
www.clcpublications.com

UK: Kingsway CLC Trust
Unit 5, Glendale Avenue, Sandycroft, Flintshire, CH5 2QP
www.equippingthechurch.com

Printed in the United States of America

ISBN (paperback): 978-1-61958-251-4
ISBN (e-book): 978-1-61958-252-1

Unless otherwise noted, all Scripture quotations are from the Holy Bible, New King James Version, copyright © 1979, 1980, 1982 by Thomas Nelson, Inc. Used by permission. All rights reserved.

Scripture quotations marked KJV are from the Holy Bible, King James Version, 1611.

Scripture quotations marked ASV are from the Holy Bible, American Standard Version, 1901.

Italics in Scripture quotations are the emphasis of the author.

Cover design by Mitch Bolton.

FOREWORD

THESE chapters were written by my father some time before his last illness. They were meant as a message to missionaries all over the world, the idea of such a special message having arisen in connection with some articles in *The International Review of Missions* that dealt with various problems common to many of the Lord's servants. The thrust of these articles was the difficulty, because of the pressures of the work, of finding time for quiet, uninterrupted communion with God. But the problem is by no means limited to missionaries.

It has been my privilege and pleasure revise and arrange the order of the chapters in the manuscript on the subject. May God abundantly bless *The Secret of the Abiding Presence* to those for whom it was written, and to all readers of the little book.

ANDREW MURRAY

The Abiding Presence

"I am with you always, even to the end of the age."
Matthew 28:20

WHEN the Lord chose His twelve disciples, it was "that they might be with Him and that He might send them out to preach" (Mark 3:14). A life in fellowship with Him prepared them for the work of preaching.

So deeply were the disciples conscious of this great privilege, that when Christ spoke of His leaving them to go to the Father their hearts were filled with great sorrow. The presence of Christ had become indispensable to them; they could not think of living without Him. To comfort them, Christ gave them the promise of the Holy Spirit, assuring them of His heavenly presence in a sense far deeper and more intimate than they ever had known on earth. The law of their first calling remained unchanged: their unbroken fellowship with Him was the secret of their power to preach and to testify of Him.

When Christ gave them the Great Commission to go into all the world and preach the gospel to every creature, He added the words, "I am with you always, even to the end of the age."

The same principle stands for all His servants, for all time: without the experience of His presence with us, our preaching has no power. The secret of our strength is the living testimony that Jesus Christ is every moment with us, inspiring, directing and strengthening us. This is what made the disciples so bold in preaching Him as the Crucified One in the midst of His enemies. They never for a moment regretted His bodily absence, for they had Him with them, and in them, in the divine power of the Holy Spirit.

In all the work of the minister and the missionary, everything depends on the consciousness, through a living faith, of the abiding presence of the Lord with His servant. The living experience of the presence of Jesus is an essential element in preaching the gospel. If this becomes clouded, work becomes a human effort, without the freshness and power of the heavenly life. Nothing can bring back the power and blessing but a return to the Master's feet so that He may breathe into the heart, in divine power, His blessed word, "I am with you always!"

The Omnipotence of Christ

"All authority has been given to Me in heaven and on Earth."

Matthew 28:18

BEFORE Christ gave His disciples the Great Commission, to bring His gospel to every creature, He first revealed Himself in His divine power as a partner with God Himself, the Almighty One. It was their faith in this that enabled the disciples to undertake the work in all simplicity and boldness. They had begun to know Him in that mighty resurrection power which had conquered sin and death; there was nothing too great for Him to command or for them to undertake.

Every disciple of Jesus Christ who desires to take part in the victory that overcomes the world needs time, faith and the Holy Spirit to convince him that, as the servant of the omnipotent Lord Jesus, he is to take part in the work. He is to count literally upon the daily experience of being "strong in the Lord and in the power of His might" (Eph. 6:10). The word of promise gives the courage to obey implicitly the word of command.

Just think of what the disciples had come to know of the power of Christ Jesus here on earth! Yet that was a little thing compared to the greater works that He was now to do in and through them (see John 14:12). He has the power to work even in the feeblest of His servants with the strength of the almighty God. He has power even to use their apparent impotence to carry out His purposes. He has the power over every enemy and every human heart, over every difficulty and danger.

But remember that this power is never meant to be experienced as if it were our own. It is only as Jesus Christ as a living Person dwells and works with His divine energy in our own hearts and lives that there can be power in our preaching as a personal testimony. When Christ said to Paul, "My strength is made perfect in weakness" (2 Cor. 12:9), Paul could say what he had never learned to say before: "When I am weak, then am I strong" (12:10). The disciple of Christ who understands that all power has been entrusted by the Father to Jesus Christ, to be received from Him hour by hour, will feel the need and experience the power of that precious word, "I am with you always"—I, the Almighty One.

The Omnipresence of Christ

"I will certainly be with you."

Exodus 3:12

THE first thing that comes to a human's mind when thinking of a god is power, however limited. And the first thought about the true God is His omnipotence: "I am God Almighty" (Gen. 35:11). The second thought in Scripture is His omnipresence. God promises His servants that His unseen presence is with them. To His "I am with you," their faith responds, "You are with me."

When Christ said to His disciples, "All authority [power, KJV] has been given to Me in heaven and on earth" (Matt. 28:18), He immediately followed with the promise, "I am with you always" (28:20). The Omnipotent One is surely the Omnipresent One.

The writer of Psalm 139 speaks of God's omnipresence as something beyond his comprehension: "Such knowledge is too wonderful for me; it is high, I cannot attain it" (139:6).

The revelation of God's omnipresence in the man Christ Jesus makes the mystery still deeper. It also makes the grace that enables us to claim this presence as our strength and our joy something inexpressibly blessed. Yet many a servant of Christ finds it difficult to understand all that is implied in this promise and how it can become his daily, practical experience.

Here, as elsewhere in the spiritual life, everything depends on faith—accepting Christ's word as a divine reality and trusting the Holy Spirit to make it true to us from moment to moment. When Christ says "always" (literally, "all the days"), He means to assure us that we need not have a day of our life without that blessed presence with us. And "all the days" implies, also, "all the day." There need not be a moment without that presence. It does not depend on what we do, but on what He does. The omnipotent Christ is the omnipresent Christ; the ever-present is the everlasting, unchangeable One. And as surely as He is the unchangeable One, His presence—the power of an endless life—will be with each of His servants who trusts Him for it.

Our attitude must be a quiet, restful faith, a humble, lowly dependence on the word, "Rest in the Lord, and wait patiently for Him" (Ps. 37:7).

"I am with you always." Let our faith in Christ, the Omnipresent One, be in the quiet confidence that He will every day and every moment keep us as the apple of His eye, keep us in perfect peace, and in the sure experience of all the light and the strength we need in His service.

Day 4

Christ the Savior of the World

"This is indeed the Christ, the Savior of the world."

John 4:42

OMNIPOTENCE and omnipresence are what are called natural attributes of God. They have their true worth only when linked to and inspired by His moral attributes, holiness and love. When our Lord spoke of having been given all power in earth and heaven (omnipotence) and His presence with each of His disciples (omnipresence), His words pointed to that which lies at the root of everything: His divine glory as the Savior of the world and Redeemer of men. It was because He humbled Himself and became obedient to death on a cross that God so highly exalted Him. As the man Christ Jesus, He shared in the attributes of God because of His perfect obedience to the will of God in accomplishing the redemption of man.

This is what gives meaning and worth to what He says of Himself as the omnipotent and omnipresent One. Between His mention of these two attributes, He gives the command to go into all the world and preach the gospel and teach men to obey all that He has commanded. It is as the Redeemer who saves and keeps from sin, as the Lord Christ who claims obedience to all that He has commanded, that He promises His divine presence to be with His servants.

It follows as a matter of necessity that only when His servants show in their lives that they obey Him in all His commands can they expect the fullness of His power and His presence to be with them. Only when they themselves are living witnesses to the reality of His power to save and to keep from sin can they expect to experience His abiding presence, and the power to train others to the life of obedience that He asks.

It is Jesus Christ, the one who saves His people from their sin and enables them to say, "I delight to do Your will, O my God" (Ps. 40:8), who says, "I am with you always." The abiding presence of the Savior from sin is promised to all who have accepted Him in the fullness of His redeeming power and who preach by their lives as well as by their words what a wonderful Savior He is.

Christ Crucified

But God forbid that I should boast except in the cross of our Lord Jesus Christ, by whom the world has been crucified to me, and I to the world.

Galatians 6:14

CHRIST'S highest glory is His cross. It was in this that He glorified the Father, and the Father glorified Him. In that wonderful fifth chapter of Revelation, it is the slain Lamb in the midst of the throne who receives the worship of the ransomed and the angels and all creation.

And His servants have learned to say, "God forbid that I should boast [glory, KJV] except in the cross of our Lord Jesus Christ, by whom the world has been crucified to me, and I to the world" (6:14). Is it not reasonable that Christ's highest glory should be our only glory too?

When the Lord Jesus said to His disciples, "I am with you always," it was as the Crucified One, who had shown them His hands and His feet, that He gave this promise. And to each one who seeks to claim His promise, it is of the first importance that he should realize that it is the crucified Jesus who offers to be with me every day.

Could one reason why we find it so difficult to expect and enjoy the abiding presence be because we do not glory in the cross by which we are crucified to the world? We have been crucified with Christ; our "old man is crucified with Him" (Rom. 6:6); "those who are Christ's have crucified the flesh with its passions and desires"

(Gal. 5:24). Yet how little we have learned that the world has been crucified to us and that we are free from its power. How little we have learned, as those who are crucified with Christ, to deny ourselves, to have the mind that was in Christ when He emptied Himself and took the form of a servant, then humbled Himself and became obedient even to the death of the cross (see Phil. 2:7–8).

Let us learn the lesson that it is the crucified Christ who comes to walk with us every day and in whose power we too are to live the life that can declare, "I have been crucified with Christ; Christ crucified lives in me" (see Gal. 2:20).

Christ Glorified

For the Lamb who is in the midst of the throne will shepherd them. . . . These are the ones who follow the Lamb wherever He goes.

Revelation 7:17; 14:4

WHO is it who says, "I am with you always" (Matt. 28:20)? If He offers to be with us throughout the day, we must take time to get to know Him, so we can understand what to expect from Him. Who is He? None other than the Lamb that was slain, standing in the center of the throne! The Lamb in His deepest humiliation is now enthroned in the glory of God. This is the one who invites me to have close fellowship with and likeness to Him.

It takes time and calls for deep reverence and adoring worship to fully realize that He who dwells in the glory of the Father, before whom all heaven bows in prostrate adoration, is none other than the One who offers to be my companion, to lead me like a shepherd—a shepherd who cares for each of His sheep—so that I might be one of those who follow the Lamb wherever He goes.

Read and re-read the wonderful fifth chapter of Revelation, until your heart is possessed by this one great thought: all heaven falls prostrate, the elders cast their crowns before the throne, and the Lamb reigns in the midst of the praises and love of His ransomed ones and of all creation.

If this is He who offers to walk with me in my daily life, to be my strength, my joy and my almighty Keeper, surely I cannot expect Him to abide with me unless I bow my heart in a still deeper reverence, if possible, and in surrender to a life of such praise and service as is worthy of the love that has redeemed me.

The Lamb in the center of the throne is the embodiment of the love and omnipotent glory of the everlasting God. With this Lamb of God as your almighty Shepherd and your faithful Keeper, the thoughts and cares of earth need not prevail and separate you from His love for a single moment.

The Great Question

"Do you believe that I am able to do this?"
They said to Him, "Yes, Lord."

Matthew 9:28

I F you can believe, all things are possible to him who
believes.' Immediately the father of the child cried out
and said with tears, 'Lord, I believe; help my unbelief!'"
(Mark 9:23–24). "Jesus said . . . 'He who believes in Me,
though he may die, he shall live. . . . Do you believe this?'
She said to Him, 'Yes, Lord, I believe'" (John 11:25–27).

Because of what we have seen and heard of Christ
Jesus, our heart is ready, in answer to His question, to say
with Martha: "Yes, Lord, I believe that You are the Christ,
the Son of God." But when it comes to believing Christ's
promise of the power of the resurrection life—of His
abiding presence every day and all the day—we do not
find it so easy to declare, "I believe that this omnipotent,
omnipresent, unchangeable Christ, our Redeemer God,
will walk with me all the day, and give me the unceasing
consciousness of His holy presence." It seems to be too
strong a statement. And yet it is just this faith for which
Christ asks and which He is waiting to work within us.

We need to clearly understand the conditions under which Christ offers to reveal to us the secret of His
abiding presence. God cannot force His blessings on us
against our will. He seeks in every possible way to stir our
desire and help us realize that He is able and willing to

fulfill His promises. The resurrection of Christ from the dead is His great plea, His all-prevailing argument. If He can raise Christ, who died under the burden of all our sin and curse, surely He can, now that Christ has conquered death and is to us the Resurrection and the Life, fulfill in our hearts His promise that Christ can be so with us and so in us that He Himself is our life all the day.

So now the great question comes: In view of what we have said and seen about Christ as our Lord, as our redeeming God, are we willing to take His word in all simplicity in its divine fullness of meaning and to rest in the promise, "I am with you all the day"? Christ's question comes to us individually: "Do you believe this?" Let us not rest until we have bowed before Him and said, "Yes, Lord, I believe."

Christ Manifesting Himself

"He who has My commandments and keeps them, it is he who loves Me. And he who loves Me will be loved by My Father, and I will love him and manifest Myself to him."

John 14:21

CHRIST promised the disciples that the Holy Spirit would come to reveal His continual presence with them. When the Spirit came, Christ manifested Himself to them through the Spirit. They knew Him in a new, divine, spiritual way; they knew Him in the power of the Spirit, and had Him far more intimately and unceasingly with them than they ever had upon earth.

The condition of this revelation of Himself is comprised in the one word—love: "He who has My commandments and keeps them, it is he who loves Me. And he who loves Me will be loved by My Father, and I will love him." It is the meeting of divine and human love. The love with which Christ loved them had taken possession of their hearts and would show itself in a love characterized by full and absolute obedience. The Father would see this, and His love would rest upon that soul. Christ would then love him with the special love drawn out by the loving heart and would manifest Himself. The love of heaven shed abroad in the heart would be met by a new and blessed revelation of Christ Himself.

But this is not all. When the question was asked, "Lord, how is it that You will manifest Yourself to us?"

(John 14:22), the answer came in the repetition of the words, "If anyone loves Me, he will keep My word"; and then again, "My Father will love him, and We will come to him and make Our home with him" (14:23). In the heart thus prepared by the Holy Spirit, showing itself in the obedience of love in a fully surrendered life, the Father and the Son will take up residence.

And now, nothing less is what Christ promises them: "I am with you always." "With" implies "in"—Christ with the Father, dwelling in the heart by faith. I wish that everyone who wanted to enter into the secret of the abiding presence—"I am with you always"—would study, believe, and claim in childlike simplicity the blessed promise, "I will manifest Myself to him."

Mary: the Morning Watch

Jesus said to her, "Mary!" She turned and said to Him,
"Rabboni!" (which is to say, Teacher).

John 20:16

HERE we have the first manifestation of the risen
Savior to Mary Magdalene, the woman who loved
much.

Think of what the morning watch meant to Mary.
It is proof of the intense longing of her love that she
would not rest until she had found the Lord. It meant
separating herself from everyone else, even from the chief
of the apostles, in her longing to find Christ. It meant
struggling against fear with a faith that refused to let go
of the wonderful promise. It meant that Christ came and
fulfilled the promise: "If anyone loves Me, he will keep
My word . . . and I will love him and manifest Myself
to him" (14:23, 21). It meant that her love was met by
the love of Jesus, and she found Him, the living Lord,
in all the power of His resurrection life. It meant that
she now understood what He had said about ascending
to the Father, to the life of divine and omnipotent glory.
It meant, too, that she received marching orders from
her Lord to go and tell His brethren what she had heard
from Him.

That first morning watch of the disciples, as they
waited for the risen Lord to reveal Himself (see Matt.
28:16), was a prophecy and pledge of what a morning

devotional time is for many of us. In fear and doubt, yet with a burning love and strong hope, they waited until He whom they had barely known (because of their feeble human minds) breathed on them in the power of His resurrection life and manifested Himself as the Lord of glory. There they learned, not in words or thought but in the reality of a divine experience, what it meant to have the One who had been given all power in earth and heaven as an abiding presence.

And what are we now to learn? That nothing is a greater attraction to our Lord than the love that sacrifices everything and is satisfied with nothing less than Himself. It is to such a love that Christ manifests Himself. He loved us and gave Himself for us. Christ's love needs our love in which to reveal itself. It is to our love that He speaks the word: "I am with you always." It is love that accepts and rejoices in and lives in that word.

Emmaus: the Evening Prayer

*But they constrained Him, saying, "Abide with us" . . . And
He went in to stay with them. . . . [and] He took bread,
blessed and broke it, and gave it to them. Then their eyes
were opened and they knew Him.*

Luke 24:29–31

IF Mary teaches us how the morning watch can reveal
Jesus to us, the two disciples on the Emmaus road in
Luke 24 remind us of the place that evening prayer can
have in preparing for the full manifestation of Christ in
the soul.

To these disciples, the day had begun in thick darkness. When the women told of seeing an angel who said
Jesus was alive, they didn't know what to think. When
"Jesus Himself drew near" their eyes were "restrained" and
they didn't recognize Him (24:15, 16). How often Jesus
comes near to show Himself to us, but we are so slow of
heart to believe what the Word has declared.

But as the Lord spoke with them their hearts began
to burn within them, even though they never thought
it might be Him. It is often the same today: the Word
becomes precious to us in the fellowship of the saints;
our hearts are stirred with a new vision of what Christ's
presence may be, and yet our eyes are restrained, and we
fail to see Him.

When the Lord acted as though He would have
gone farther, their request, "Abide with us," constrained

Him. Christ had given, in the last night, a new meaning to the word "Abide." They did not yet understand that, but in their use of it they received far more than they expected—a foretaste of the life of abiding which the resurrection now made possible.

We need to learn to pause toward the close of the day, perhaps leaving the fellowship of others, and with our whole heart take up anew the promise of the abiding presence, praying with an urgency that constrains Jesus—"Abide with us."

What is now the chief lesson of this story? What led our Lord to reveal Himself to these two men? Nothing less than this: their intense devotion to their Lord. Despite our ignorance and unbelief, if we have a burning desire that longs for Him above everything else, a desire that is fostered by the Word, we may count on Him to make Himself known to us. To such intense devotion and constraining prayer the Lord's message will be given in power: "I am with you always." Our eyes will be opened, and we will know Him and the blessed secret of the always-abiding presence. It is to strong desire and constraining prayer that Christ is certain to reveal Himself.

The Disciples: Their Divine Mission

Then, the same day at evening . . . when the doors were shut where the disciples were assembled, for fear of the Jews, Jesus came and stood in the midst, and said to them, "Peace be with you."

John 20:19

THE disciples had received the message of Mary. Peter also said that he had seen the Lord. Late in the evening the men from Emmaus told how He had been made known to them. Their hearts were prepared for what now came, when Jesus stood in their midst and said, "Peace be with you," and showed them His hands and feet. This was not only a sign of recognition; it was also the deep eternal mystery of what would be seen in heaven when He was exalted to the throne: "a Lamb as though it had been slain" (Rev. 5:6).

John goes on to say that "the disciples were glad when they saw the Lord" (John 20:20). And He spoke again: "Peace to you! As the Father has sent Me, I also send you" (20:21). With Mary, He had revealed Himself to the fervent love that could not rest without Him. With the men at Emmaus it was their constraining prayer that received the revelation. Here, now, He meets the willing servants whom He had trained for His service and hands over to them the work He had done on earth. He changes their fear into the boldness of peace and gladness. He later on ascends to the Father; the work the Father had given Him to do He entrusts to them. The divine mission is now theirs to make known and carry out to victory. For this divine work they will need nothing less than divine power. He breathes upon them the resurrection life He had won by His death. He fulfills the promise He gave: "Because I live, you will live also" (John 14:19). The exceeding greatness of the mighty power of God by which He raised Christ from the dead—none other than that Spirit of holiness by which He, as the Son of God, was resurrected—will now work in them! And all that is bound or loosed by them in that power will be bound or loosed in heaven.

The story comes to every messenger of the gospel with soul-stirring force. To us, too, the word has been spoken: "As the Father has sent Me, I also send you." For us, too, is the word "Receive the Holy Spirit" (20:22); for us, too, is Jesus revealed as the Living One, with the pierced hands and feet. If our hearts are set on nothing less than the presence of the living Lord, we may confidently count that it will be given to us. Jesus never sends His servants out without the promise of His abiding presence and His almighty power.

Thomas: the Blessedness of Believing

Jesus said to him, "Thomas, because you have seen Me, you have believed. Blessed are those who have not seen and yet have believed."

John 20:29

WE all think Thomas received a wonderful blessing: Christ appeared and allowed Thomas to touch His hands and side. No wonder he could find no words but those of holy adoration: "My Lord and my God" (20:28). Has there ever been a higher expression of the overwhelming nearness and glory of God?

And yet Christ said: "Because you have seen Me, you have believed. Blessed are those who have not seen and yet have believed." True, living faith gives a sense of Christ's divine nearness far deeper and more intimate than even the joy that filled the heart of Thomas. Here and now, after all these centuries, we can experience the presence and power of Christ in a far deeper reality than Thomas did. To those who have not seen, yet believe—simply, only, truly, fully believe in what Christ is and can be to them every moment—He has promised to reveal Himself, and the Father and He will come and dwell in them.

How often have you been inclined to think of a "full life of faith" as something beyond your reach? Such a thought robs you of the power to believe. Instead, take hold of Christ's word: "Blessed are those who have not seen, and yet have believed." This is a heavenly blessing that fills the whole heart and life—a faith that receives the love and the presence of the living Lord.

How do you obtain this childlike faith? The answer is very simple: If Jesus Christ is the sole object of your desire and your confidence, He will reveal Himself in divine power. Thomas had already proved his intense devotion to Christ when he said, "Let us also go, that we may die with Him" (John 11:16). To such a love, even when it is struggling with unbelief, Jesus Christ will reveal Himself. He will make His holy promise "I am with you always" an actual reality in our conscious experience. See to it that your faith in His blessed word, His divine power, and His holy, abiding presence is the one thing that masters your whole being. Then Christ is sure to reveal Himself, abide with you and dwell in your heart as His home.

Peter: the Greatness of Love

*Peter was grieved because He said to him the third time,
"Do you love Me?" And he said to Him, "Lord, You know all
things; You know that I love You." Jesus said to him,
"Feed My sheep."*

John 21:17

IT was to Mary who "loved much" that Christ first revealed Himself. Likewise, when He appeared to Peter,
to the two disciples in the supper room at Emmaus, to the
ten and to Thomas, it was always to the intense devotion
of prepared hearts that Christ revealed Himself. And in
His second appearance to Peter, love is again the keynote.

We can easily understand why Christ asked the
question, "Do you love Me?" three times. It was to
remind Peter of the terrible self-confidence in which
he had said, "Even if I have to die with You, I will not
deny You" (Matt. 26:35). It was because of his need for
quiet, deep heart-searching before he could be sure that
his love was real and true. It was because he needed to
be deeply penitent and realize how little he could trust
himself. Love was the one thing Peter needed to be fully
restored to his place in the heart of Jesus—the first and
highest requirement for feeding His sheep and caring
for His lambs.

God is love. Christ is the Son of His love. Having
loved His own, He loved them to the uttermost, and
said: "As the Father loved Me, I also have loved you"

(John 15:9). He asked them to prove their love to Him by keeping His commandments and loving each other with the love with which He loved them. In heaven and on earth, in the Father and in the Son, in us and all our work for Him, and especially in our care for souls, the greatest thing is love.

To everyone who longs to have Jesus reveal Himself—as in "I am with you always"—the essential requirement is love. Peter teaches us that such love is not in our power to offer. It comes to us through the power of Christ's death to sin, and of His resurrection life. As he puts it in his first epistle, "Whom having not seen you love. Though now you do not see Him, yet believing, you rejoice with joy inexpressible and full of glory" (1 Pet. 1:8). Thank God, if Peter, the self-confident, could be so changed, can we not believe that Christ will work this wondrous change in us, too? He reveals Himself to a loving heart in all the fullness of His precious declaration, "I am with you always." It is to love that Christ reveals Himself, and only those who love are fit to feed His sheep and tend His lambs.

John: Life from the Dead

*And when I saw Him, I fell at His feet as dead. But He laid
His right hand on me, saying to me, "Do not be afraid; I am
the First and the Last. I am He who lives, and was dead,
and behold, I am alive forevermore. Amen."*

Revelation 1:17–18

HERE we see, sixty or more years after the resurrection, Christ revealing Himself to the beloved disciple. John fell as dead at His feet. When Moses prayed,
"Show me Your glory," God said, "You cannot see My
face; for no man shall see Me, and live" (Exod. 33:18,
20). Man's sinful nature cannot receive the vision of the
divine glory and live; it needs the death of the natural
life for the life of God in glory to enter in. When John
fell as dead at Christ's feet, it proved how little he could
endure the wonderful heavenly vision.

When Christ laid His right hand upon him and
said, "Do not be afraid . . . I am He who lives, and was
dead, and behold, I am alive forevermore," He reminded
him that He Himself, too, had passed through death
before He could rise to the life and the glory of God.
For the Master Himself and for every disciple, for Moses
and for John, there is only one way to the glory of God:
death to all that has been in contact with sin and cannot
enter heaven.

The lesson is a deep and necessary one for all who
long for Jesus to reveal Himself to them. Deep knowledge

of Jesus—fellowship with Him and the experience of His power—is not possible without sacrificing all that is in us of the world and its spirit. The disciples had personal experience of this. From His first ordination charge, where He spoke about forsaking father and mother, taking up the cross and losing our life for His sake (see Matt. 10:37–39), down to the days before His death, when He said, "Unless a grain of wheat falls into the ground and dies, it remains alone; but if it dies, it produces much grain," and "He who loves his life will lose it" (John 12:24–25), Christ made this His one great command: deny yourself, bear the cross, and follow Me (see Matt. 16:24). The secret of having the Lord Jesus' daily abiding presence is accepting the principle of "through death to life." In the power of Christ Jesus—with whom we have been crucified, and whose death now works in us if we yield ourselves to it—*death* to sin and to the world, with all its self-pleasing and self-exaltation, must be the deepest law of our spiritual life. Peter advised Jesus to spare Himself from the cross. Jesus said to him, "Deny yourself" (see 16:22, 24). The disciples followed Christ even to the cross. That was what made them fit to receive the Master's word, "I am with you always."

Paul: Christ Revealed in Him

But . . . it pleased God . . . to reveal His Son in me.
Galatians 1:15–16

IN all our study and worship of Christ, five points come to mind: the Incarnate Christ, the Crucified Christ, the Enthroned Christ, the Indwelling Christ and Christ Coming in Glory. The first is the seed, the second the seed cast into the ground and the third the seed growing up to heaven. The fourth is the fruit: Christ dwelling in the heart through the Holy Spirit. The fifth is the gathering of the fruit when Christ appears.

Paul tells us that it pleased God to reveal His Son in him (see 1:15–16). And he gives his testimony of that revelation: "Christ lives in me" (2:20). The main aspect of that life, he says, is that he is crucified with Christ and is able to say, "I no longer live." In Christ he had found the death of self.

Just as the cross is the chief characteristic of Christ Himself—"A lamb as though it had been slain" (Rev. 5:6)—so the life of Christ in Paul made him inseparably one with his crucified Lord. So completely was this the case that he could say, "But God forbid that I should boast except in the cross of our Lord Jesus Christ, by whom the world has been crucified to me, and I to the world" (Gal. 6:14).

Suppose you had asked Paul, "If Christ actually lives in you, so that you no longer live, what becomes of your responsibility?" His answer was ready and clear: "I live by faith in the Son of God, who loved me and gave Himself for me" (Gal. 2:20). Every moment he lived was a life of faith in the One who loved him and gave Himself so completely that He had undertaken at all times to be the life of His willing disciple.

This was the sum and substance of all Paul's preaching. He asks for intercession that he might proclaim "this mystery among the Gentiles: which is Christ in you, the hope of glory" (Col. 1:27). The indwelling Christ was the secret of his life of faith; the one power, the one aim of all his life and work; the hope of glory. We can be sure that the abiding presence of Christ is given to everyone who trusts Him fully.

Why Could We Not?

Then the disciples came to Jesus privately and said, "Why could we not cast it out?" So Jesus said to them, "Because of your unbelief. . . . However, this kind does not go out except by prayer and fasting."

Matthew 17:19–21

THE disciples had often cast out demons, but now they had been unable to do so. They asked the Lord what the reason might be. His answer is very simple: "Because of your unbelief."

We have here the reply to the great question so often asked, "How is it that we cannot live that life of unbroken fellowship with Christ which the Scripture promises?" Simply, because of our unbelief. We do not realize that faith must accept and expect that God will, by His almighty power, fulfill every promise He has made. We do not live in that utter helplessness and dependence on God alone which is the very essence of faith. We are not strong in our faith, fully persuaded that what God has promised He is able and willing to perform. We do not give ourselves with our whole heart simply to believe that God by His almighty power will work wonders in our hearts.

But what is the reason that this faith is so often lacking? "However, this kind does not go out except by prayer and fasting." To have a strong faith in God demands a life in close touch with Him by persistent prayer. We cannot call up faith on our own; it requires close intercourse with God. It requires not only prayer but fasting too, in the larger and deeper meaning of that word. It requires the denial of self—giving up "the lust of the flesh, the lust of the eyes, and the pride of life" (1 John 2:16), which is the essence of a worldly spirit. To gain the prizes of the heavenly life here on earth calls for the sacrifice of all that earth can offer. Just as it takes God to satisfy the human heart and work His mighty miracles in it, it takes the whole man, utterly given up to God, to have the faith which can cast out every evil spirit. "Prayer and fasting" are essential.

The Power of Obedience

"And He who sent Me is with Me. The Father has not left Me alone, for I always do those things that please Him."

John 8:29

IN these words Christ not only tells what *His* life with the Father was like, but reveals at the same time the law of *all* intercourse with God—simple obedience.

How strongly He insisted upon it is seen in His Farewell Discourse (see 14–16). In chapter 14 He says three times that loving Him means keeping His commandments (see 14:15, 21, 23). And likewise three times over in chapter 15 he connects our love to Him with abiding in His word, or obeying Him (see 15:7, 10, 14).

Obedience is the proof and practice of the love of God that has been poured out in our hearts by the Holy Spirit. Obedience comes from love and leads to love—a deeper and a fuller experience of God's love and indwelling. It assures us that what we ask will be given to us. It assures us that we are abiding in the love of Christ. It seals our claim to be called the friends of Christ. And so it is not only a proof of love but of faith too, since we are promised that "whatever we ask we receive from Him, because we keep His commandments and do those things that are pleasing in His sight" (1 John 3:22).

To have the abiding enjoyment of His holy presence, simple, full obedience is necessary. The new covenant has made full provision for this: "I will . . . write [My law] on their hearts" (Jer. 31:33); "I will put My fear in their hearts so that they will not depart from Me" (32:40); "I will put My Spirit within you and cause you to walk in My statutes, and you will keep My judgments and do them" (Ezek. 36:27).

Blessed obedience, that enables us to abide in His love and gives the full experience of His unbroken presence! Christ did not speak of an impossibility; He saw what we might confidently expect in the power of the Spirit. Let this thought take deep hold of you: to the obedient comes the promise, "I am with you always," and to them all the fullness of its meaning will be revealed.

The Power of Intercession

"We will give ourselves continually to prayer."

Acts 6:4

Constant prayer was offered to God for him by the church.

12:5

WHILE traveling in Asia, Dr. John R. Mott was urged by missionaries there to remind us of the imperative need for more intercession—above all, of united intercession.

"We can in no way better serve the deepest interest of the churches than by multiplying the number of real intercessors, and by focusing the prayers of Christendom upon those great situations which demand the almighty working of the Spirit of God," Dr. Mott said. "Far more important and vital than any service we can render to missions is that of helping to release the superhuman energy of prayer, and, through uniting true intercessors of all lands in this holy ministry, to help usher in a new era abounding in signs and wonders. . . . Immeasurably more important than any other work is the linking of all we do to the fountain of divine life and energy."

And where is there a greater need of focusing the united intercession of Christendom than on the great army of missionaries? They confess the need of the presence and the power of God's Spirit in their life and work. They long for the experience of the abiding presence and the power of Christ every day. They need it; they have a right to it. Will you be a part of that great army which pleads with God for that enduement of power which is so absolutely necessary for effective work? Will you, like the early apostles, continue steadfastly in prayer (see Acts 2:42) until God sends an abundant answer?

As we give ourselves continually to prayer, the power of Christ's promise, "I am with you always," will be proved in our lives and in theirs.

The Power of Time

My times are in Your hand.

Psalm 31:15

THE plural implies the singular: "My time is in Your hand. It belongs to You; You alone have a right to command it. I yield it wholly and gladly to Your disposal." What mighty power time can exert if wholly given up to God!

Time is the lord of all things. What is the history of the world but a proof of how, slowly but surely, time has made man what he is today? All around us we see the proof—in the growth of a child to physical and mental adulthood, in the success of every pursuit, in all our endeavors and attainments. All these are under the law of time and its inconceivable power over how we spend our lives.

This is especially true in spiritual matters and one's intercourse with God. Time here, too, is master. What glorious fellowship with God! What holiness and blessedness! What likeness to His image and what power in His service for blessing to men! All these benefits we can obtain on one condition: that we have sufficient time with God for His holiness to shine on us with its light and heat and make us partakers of His Spirit and His life. The very essence of religion lies in the concept of time with God. And yet many of God's servants, even while giving their lives to His service, frankly admit to feebleness in their spiritual life and to inadequate results in their work as a whole, due to a failure to set aside time and use it rightly in daily communion with God.

The cause behind this sad situation is nothing but a lack of faith—a failure to believe that time spent alone with God truly will bring power into our lives and enable us to use our time wisely and enjoy His abiding presence with us all the day.

If you are complaining that overwork, or too much zeal in doing the work, is hindering your spiritual efficiency, submit your timetable to the inspection of Christ and His Holy Spirit, and you will find that a new life will be yours. You must fully believe and then put into daily practice the word, "My time is in Your hand."

The Power of Faith

"All things are possible to him who believes."

Mark 9:23

THERE is no truth that Christ insisted on more frequently, both with His disciples and with strangers who came seeking His help, than the absolute necessity of faith, with its unlimited possibilities. And experience has taught us that there is nothing in which we fall so short as a simple and absolute trust in God to fulfill literally, in us, all that He has promised. To have a life in the abiding presence requires a life of unceasing faith.

Think for a moment of what the marks of true faith are. First of all, faith counts on God to do all He has promised. It is not content with taking hold of some promises; it seeks nothing less than to claim every promise that God has made and does so in its largest and fullest meaning. Sensing its own nothingness and utter impotence, it trusts the power of an almighty God to work His wonders in the heart in which He dwells.

It does this wholeheartedly and with all its strength. Faith yields to the promise that God will take full possession of the believer and, all through the day and night, fulfill his hope and expectation. It recognizes the inseparable link between God's promises and His commands, and submits to doing the one as fully as it trusts the other.

In pursuit of the power which such a life of faith can give, there is often a faith that seeks and strives, but cannot grasp. This is then followed by a faith that begins to see the need to wait on God, and it quietly rests in the hope of what God will do. This should lead to an act of decision in which the soul takes God at His word and claims the fulfillment of the promise, looking to Him even in utter darkness to perform what He has spoken.

The kind of faith which leads to the abiding presence demands a mastery of one's whole being. Experiencing Christ's presence all day long is such a wonderful privilege that it calls us to forsake many things we formerly thought were lawful. The blessed Friend who accompanies us, the joy and light of our life, must be Lord of all. Then faith will be able to claim and experience the words of the Master, "I am with you always."

John's Missionary Message

That which we have seen and heard we declare to you, that you also may have fellowship with us; and truly our fellowship is with the Father and with His Son Jesus Christ.

1 John 1:3

WHAT a revelation of the calling of the preacher of the gospel! His message is nothing less than to proclaim that Christ has opened the way for us simple men to have daily, living, loving fellowship with the holy God! He is to preach this as a witness to the life he himself lives in all its blessed experience. In the power of that testimony he is to prove its reality, and to show how a sinful man upon earth can indeed live in fellowship with the Father and the Son.

The message suggests that the very first duty of a pastor or missionary is to maintain such close communion with God that he can preach the truth in fullness of joy, and with a consciousness that his life and conversation are proof that his preaching is true, so that his words appeal with power to the heart. "And these things we write to you that your joy may be full" (1:4).

In an article in *The International Review of Missions* of October 1914, on the influence of the Keswick Convention on mission work, the substance of Keswick teaching is given in these words: "It points to a life of communion with God through Christ as a reality to be entered upon, and constantly maintained, by the unconditional and habitual surrender of the whole personality to Christ's control and government, in the assurance that the living Christ will take possession of the life thus yielded to Him." It is such teaching, revealing the infinite claim and power of Christ's love as maintained by the power of the Holy Spirit, that will encourage and compel men to make the measure of Christ's surrender for them the only measure of their surrender to Him and His service.

It is this intimate fellowship with Christ (as the secret of daily service and testimony) that has power to make Christ known as the deliverer from sin and the inspiration of a life of wholehearted devotion to His service.

This intimate and abiding fellowship with Christ is promised in the verse "I am with you always" (Matt. 28:20). This is what every missionary needs, and has a right to claim. This alone maintains that spiritual efficiency which will influence the workers and converts with whom he comes in contact.

Paul's Missionary Message

Continue earnestly in prayer . . . meanwhile praying also for
us, that God would open to us a door for the word, to speak
the mystery of Christ . . . that I may
make it manifest, as I ought to speak.

Colossians 4:2–4

The mystery which has been hidden . . . but now has been
revealed to His saints. To them God willed to make known
what are the riches of the glory of this mystery among the
Gentiles: which is Christ in you, the hope of glory.

1:26–27

TO Paul, the very center and substance of his gospel
was the indwelling Christ. He spoke of "the riches
of the glory of this mystery . . . Christ in you, the hope of
glory." Though he had been so many years a preacher of
this gospel, he still asked for prayer, that he might make
known that mystery clearly.

A complaint often made of churches on the mission
field is that, after a time, there appears to be no further
growth, and very little joy and power for bearing witness
to Christ Jesus. The question to be asked is whether the
missionary's church at home is living in the experience
of this indwelling Christ. If not, how can the sons and
daughters this church sends out know the secret and
make it the substance of their teaching and preaching?

Some years ago, one of our workers returned from
the mission field to do deputation work. Before he began visiting the supporting churches, there was a little

gathering for prayer at which he asked what his general message should be. The thought was expressed that since he would be speaking to Christians, it was desirable that a message of a full salvation should be pressed home and hearts be roused to believe in an indwelling Christ. Upon his return, he told what deep interest the presentation of this truth had produced; many people said they had never before rightly understood it.

Dr. Alexander Maclaren said years ago that "it seems as if the Church has lost the truth of the indwelling Christ." We speak of Paul's missionary methods, but is there not a greater need of Paul's missionary message, which culminates in the phrase, "Christ in you, the hope of glory"? Even Paul felt a great need for prayer to enable him to give the message correctly. All missionary intercessors, and our beloved missionaries themselves, should make it their top priority to obtain the power, growing from personal experience, to lead Christians into the enjoyment of their rightful heritage. And it may be that the church at home will also share in the blessing—the restoration of the truth, "Christ in you, the hope of glory" to its rightful place.

The Missionary's Life

You are witnesses, and God also, how devoutly and justly and blamelessly we behaved ourselves among you who believe.
1 Thessalonians 2:10

PAUL more than once appeals to what his converts had seen in his own life. So he says, "For our boasting is this: the testimony of our conscience that we conducted ourselves in the world in simplicity and godly sincerity, not with fleshly wisdom but by the grace of God, and more abundantly toward you" (2 Cor. 1:12). Christ, also, had taught His disciples as much by His life as by His teaching. Paul consistently sought to be a living witness to the truth of all that he had preached about Christ—as able to save and to keep from sin, as renewing the whole nature by the power of His Holy Spirit, as Himself becoming the life of those who believe in Him.

In the *W. M. C. Report* (Vol. v, p. 217) one finds this statement: "It has come to pass that our representatives on the field, just because they are what we have made them, have far too often hidden the Christ whom they are giving their lives to reveal. It is only in proportion as the missionary can manifest the character of Christ in and through his own life that he can gain a hearing for the gospel. Only as far as he can live Christ before their eyes can he help them to understand his message."

Paul's appeal to his own holy, righteous and blameless life gave him courage to put a high standard before his converts in Thessalonica. He calls on them to trust God to establish their hearts blameless in holiness before God (see 1 Thess. 3:13). And in Philippians 4:9 he writes, "The things which you . . . heard and saw in me, these do, and the God of peace will be with you." Then to Timothy he declares, "And the grace of our Lord was exceedingly abundant, with faith and love which are in Christ Jesus . . . a pattern to those who are going to believe on Him for everlasting life" (1 Tim. 1:14, 16).

When Paul said, "Christ lives in me, I live no more" (see Gal. 2:20), he spoke of an actual, divine, unceasing abiding of Christ in him, working in him from hour to hour all that was pleasing to the Father. Do not rest until you can say, "The Christ of Paul is my Christ! His missionary standard is mine, too!"

The Holy Spirit

*"He will glorify Me, for He will take of what is Mine and
declare it to you."*

John 16:14

WHEN our Lord said to the disciples, "I am with
you always," they did not at first understand or
experience His full meaning.

It was only later, at Pentecost, when they were
filled with the Holy Spirit and that Spirit from heaven
brought down into their hearts the glorified Lord Jesus,
that they could begin their new life in the joy of the
abiding presence.

All our attempts to claim that life of continuous,
unbroken communion will be in vain unless we too
yield ourselves wholly to the power and indwelling of
the ever-blessed Spirit.

Throughout the church of Christ there is an appall-
ing lack of knowledge of and faith in the Spirit—His
divine nature, what He can enable us to be, and how
completely He demands *full and undisturbed possession*
of our whole being. Clearly, the fulfillment of Christ's
glorious promises about the Father and Son making their
abode in us is subject to one essential and indispensable
condition—a life utterly and unceasingly yielded to the
rule and leading of the Spirit of Christ.

Let no one say, "The experience of Christ's being
with us every day and all the day is impossible." Christ

meant His word to be a simple and eternal *reality*. He meant these promises—"He who loves Me will be loved by My Father, and I will love him and manifest Myself to him" (John 14:21), and "We will come unto him and make our abode with him" (14:23, KJV)—to be accepted as *absolute*, divine truth. But this truth can only be experienced where the Spirit, in His power as God, is known and believed in and obeyed.

What Christ speaks of in John 14 is exactly what Paul testifies to when he says, "Christ lives in me," or, as John expressed it, "By this we know that we abide in Him, and He in us, because He has given us of His Spirit" (1 John 4:13).

Christ came as God to make known the Father, and the Spirit has come as God to make known the Son in us. We need to understand that the Spirit of God not only seeks our absolute subjection but desires, by taking possession of our whole being, to enable us to fulfill all that Christ asks of us. It is the *Spirit* who can deliver us from all the power of the flesh and who can conquer the power of the world. *He* is the One through whom Christ Jesus will reveal Himself to us in nothing less than His abiding presence: "I am with you always."

Filled with the Spirit

Be filled with the Spirit, speaking to one another in psalms
and hymns and spiritual songs, singing and making melody
in your heart to the Lord, giving thanks always for all things.
Ephesians 5:18–20

IF the expression "filled with the Spirit" related only to the story of Pentecost, we might naturally think that it was something special and not meant for ordinary life. But the text above teaches us the great lesson that it is meant for every Christian and for everyday life.

To realize this more fully, think of the Holy Spirit in Christ Jesus and the conditions under which He, as man, was filled with the Spirit. He received the Spirit while praying, having yielded Himself as a sacrifice to God by going down into the sinner's baptism. And full of the Holy Spirit He was led to forty days of fasting, sacrificing the needs of the body in order to be free for fellowship with the Father and have victory over Satan. He even refused, while hungry, to listen to the urging of the Evil One to use His power to make bread. And so He was led by the Spirit through life until He, by the Eternal Spirit, on Calvary offered Himself, without blemish, to God.

For Christ, the Spirit's filling meant prayer, obedience and sacrifice. If we are to follow Christ—to have His mind in us and live out His life—we must seek to regard the fullness of the Spirit as a daily supply, as a daily provision. Only in this way can we live a life of obedience, joy, self-sacrifice and power for service. There may be occasions when the fullness of the Spirit is especially evident, but being led by the Spirit—every day and all day—is the only way we can abide in Christ Jesus, conquer the flesh and the world and live life with God and our fellow men in humble, holy, fruitful service.

Only when we are filled with the Spirit can we fully understand and experience the words of Jesus, "I am with you always." If this seems unattainable, remember that what is impossible with men is possible with God (see Luke 18:27). And if we cannot attain to it at once, let us at least make it, in an act of holy decision, our definite aim, our unceasing prayer, our childlike expectation.

"I am with you always" was meant for daily life, with the all-sufficient aid of that blessed Spirit of whom Jesus said, "He who believes in Me . . . out of his heart will flow rivers of living water" (John 7:38). Our faith in Christ is the measure of our fullness of the Spirit. The measure of the power of the Spirit in us will be the measure of our experience of the presence of Christ.

The Christ Life

Christ lives in me.

Galatians 2:20

Christ . . . is our life.

Colossians 3:4

CHRIST'S life was more than His teaching, more than His work, more even than His death. It was His life in the sight of God and man that gave value to what He said and did and suffered. And it is this life, glorified in the resurrection, that He gives to His people, enabling them to live it out before men.

"By this all will know that you are My disciples, if you have love for one another" (John 13:35). It was the life of Christ's Spirit that made both Jews and Greeks feel that there was a superhuman power motivating the new brotherhood that came into being. They gave living proof of the truth of what they said, that God's love had come down and taken possession of them.

It has often been said of the missionary that unless he lives his life on an entirely different level from that on which other men live, he misses the deepest secret of power and success in his work. When Christ sent His disciples forth, it was with the command, "Tarry . . . until you are endued with power from on high" (Luke 24:49). Many a missionary has realized that neither learning, nor zeal, nor a willingness to sacrifice in Christ's service can promise success. It is only the secret experience of a life hidden with Christ in God that enables him to meet and overcome every difficulty.

Everything depends on our life with God in Christ being kept right. It was so with Christ, with the disciples, with Paul. It is the simplicity and intensity of our life in Christ Jesus, and of the life of Christ Jesus in us, that sustains a man in the daily drudgery of work, that makes him conqueror over self and everything that could hinder the Christ-life, and that gives victory over the powers of evil and over the hearts from which the evil spirits have to be cast out.

The life is everything. It was so in Christ Jesus; it must be so in His servants. It can be so, because Christ Himself will live in us. When He spoke the word, "I am with you always," He meant nothing less than this: "Every day and all the day I am with you, the secret of your life, joy and strength."

There are hidden treasures contained in those blessed words we love to repeat: "I am with you always."

The Christ-like Life

Let this mind be in you which was also in Christ Jesus.
Philippians 2:5

A ND what was the mind that was in Christ Jesus?
"Who, being in the form of God . . . made Himself of no reputation, taking the form of a bondservant, and coming in the likeness of men. . . . He humbled Himself and became obedient to the point of death, even the death of the cross" (2:6–8). Self-emptying and self-sacrifice, obedience to God's will and submission in love to men, even unto the death of the cross—such was the character of Christ for which God so highly exalted Him. Such is the character of Christ that we are to imitate. He was made in the likeness of men that we might be conformed into the likeness of God.

Self-effacement, self-sacrifice, to do God's will and save man—such was the life of Christ. "Love . . . does not seek its own" (1 Cor. 13:4–5). This was His life: He lived only to please God and to bless men.

This is not an impossibility. "The things which are impossible with men are possible with God" (Luke 18:27). We are called to work out this salvation of a Christ-like character with fear and trembling, for "it is God who works in you both to will and to do for His good pleasure" (Phil. 2:13).

It has been said that "the missionary who is to commend the gospel must first embody it in a character fully conformed to the likeness of Jesus Christ. It is only as far as he can live Christ before the eyes of the converts that he can help them to understand his message. It has at times come to pass that our representatives on the field, just because they are what we have made them, have far too often hidden the Christ whom they are giving their lives to reveal" (*W.M.C. Report*, Vol. v., p. 217).

As the church aims to make likeness to Christ's character the standard for Christian teachers, our missionaries are able to pass this on to their converts and say to them, as Paul said, "Imitate me, just as I also imitate Christ" (1 Cor. 11:1).

Let us not rest until our faith lays hold of the promise, "It is *God* who works in us." The confidence will be aroused that as the character of Christ is the revelation with which every missionary has been entrusted, so the power will be given to fulfill this high and holy calling. Let ministers and missionaries and all intercessors make this their one great plea and aim: to have this mind that was in Christ Jesus.

Christ: the Nearness of God

Draw near to God and He will draw near to you.

James 4:8

IT has been said that the holiness of God is the union of God's infinite distance from sinful man with God's infinite nearness in His redeeming grace. Faith must always seek to realize both the distance and the nearness.

In Christ, God has come near to man, and James tells us that if we want God to come even nearer, we must draw near to Him. The nearness that Jesus promised when He said, "I am with you always," can only be experienced as we draw near to Him.

That means, first of all, that at the beginning of each day we must yield ourselves afresh for His holy presence to rest upon us. It means a voluntary, intentional and wholehearted turning away from the world, and waiting on God to make Himself known to our souls. It means giving Him time, and all our heart and strength, to allow Him to reveal Himself. We cannot expect to have the abiding presence of Christ with us through the day unless we definitely and daily exercise a strong desire and childlike trust in His word. "Draw near to God and He will draw near to you."

That also means we must offer ourselves in simple, childlike faith to do His will alone, and to seek above everything to please Him. We can depend on His promise that "If anyone loves Me, he will keep My word; and My

Father will love him, and We will come to him and make Our home with him" (John 14:23).

This will bring a quiet assurance, even if there is not much feeling or sense of His presence, that God is with us, and that as we go out to do His will He will watch over us and keep us, strengthening us in the inner man for the work we have to do for Him.

Let these words have a new meaning for you each morning: "Draw near to God and He will draw near to you." Wait patiently, and He will speak in divine power, "I am with you always."

Love

Having loved His own who were in the world, He loved them to the end.

John 13:1

THESE are the opening words of that holy, confidential talk of Christ with His disciples in John 13 to 17, as out of the depths of eternity He discoursed with them in the last hours before He went to Gethsemane. They are the revelation and full display of that divine love which was manifested in His death on the cross.

He begins with a new commandment: "Love one another; as I have loved you" (13:34). A little later He adds, "If you love Me, keep My commandments. . . . He who loves Me will be loved by My Father, and I will love him and manifest Myself to him. . . . We will come to him and make Our home with him" (14:15, 21, 23). The new, heavenly life in Christ Jesus is to be the unfolding of God's love in Christ.

Further on He says, "As the Father loved Me, I also have loved you; abide in My love. If you keep My commandments, you will abide in My love. . . . This is My commandment, that you love one another as I have loved you. Greater love has no one than this, than to lay down one's life for his friends" (15:9–10, 12–13).

Then later He prays "that the world may know that You have sent Me, and have loved them as You have loved Me. . . . I have declared to them Your name . . . that the

The Secret of the Abiding Presence

love with which You loved Me may be in them, and I in them" (John 17:23, 26).

Can His words make it any plainer that God's love to Christ is given that it might pass into us and become our life? That the love with which the Father loved the Son is to be in us? If the Lord Jesus is to reveal Himself to us, it can only be to the loving heart. If we are to claim His daily presence with us, it can only be as a relationship of infinite, tender love between Him and us—love rooted in the fact of God's love to Christ coming into our hearts. And such love will show itself in obedience to His commandment to love one another.

We see how in the early church the "first love" was forsaken after a time, and confidence was put in all the activities of service (see Rev. 2:4). It is only in the atmosphere of a holy, living love that the abiding presence of the loving Christ can be known, and the depth of the divine love expressed in Christ's promise, "I am with you always," can be realized.

The Trial and Triumph of Faith

Jesus said to him, "If you can believe, all things are possible to him who believes." Immediately the father of the child cried out and said with tears, "Lord, I believe; help my unbelief!"

Mark 9:23–24

WHAT a glorious promise: "All things are possible to him who believes"! And yet it is the very greatness of the promise that makes it a trial of faith. At first we do not really believe its truth. But when we have grasped it, then comes the real trial, in which we think: such a wonder-working faith is utterly beyond my reach.

But the trial of faith soon becomes its triumph! How can this be? When Christ said to the father of the child, "If you can believe, all things are possible to him who believes," he felt that this was only casting him into deeper despair. How could his faith be able to work the miracle? But as he looked into the face of Christ and the love of His tender eyes touched his heart, he felt sure that this blessed Man not only had the power to heal his child but the ability, too, to inspire him with the needed faith. The impression Christ produced upon him made not only the one miracle of the healing possible but the second miracle too—that he should have so great a faith. And with tears he cried, "Lord, I believe; help my unbelief!" The very greatness of faith's trial was the greatness of faith's triumph.

What a lesson! Of all things that are possible to faith, the most impossible is that I should be able to exercise such faith. The abiding presence of Christ is possible to faith. And this faith is possible to the soul that clings to Christ and trusts Him. As surely as He will lead us into His abiding presence all the day, so surely will He strengthen us with divine power for the faith that claims and receives the promise. Blessed is the hour when the believer sees how entirely he is dependent on Christ for the faith as well as the blessing, and, in the consciousness of the unbelief that is still struggling within, he casts himself on the power and the love of Jesus: "Lord, I believe; Lord, I believe!"

Through such trial and through such triumph— sometimes the triumph of despair—we enter upon our inheritance, the abiding presence of Him who speaks to us now: "I am with you always." Let us wait at His feet until we know that He has blessed us. "I can do all things through Christ who strengthens me" (Phil. 4:13).

Exceedingly Abundantly

*Now to Him who is able to do exceedingly abundantly above
all that we ask or think, according to the power that works
in us, to Him be glory in the church by Christ Jesus to all
generations, forever and ever. Amen.*

Ephesians 3:20–21

IN Paul's great prayer (see 3:14–19), he had apparently
reached the highest expression possible regarding the
life to which God's mighty power can bring the believer.
But Paul is not content. In this doxology he rises still
higher and lifts us up to give glory to God as "able to do
exceedingly abundantly above all that we ask or think."
Pause a moment to think what "exceedingly abundantly"
means.

Think of the "exceedingly great and precious promises" (2 Peter 1:4). Think of "the exceeding greatness
of His power toward us who believe, according to the
working of His mighty power which He worked in Christ
when He raised Him from the dead" (Eph. 1:19–20).
Think of how "the grace of our Lord was exceedingly
abundant, with faith and love which are in Christ Jesus" (1 Tim. 1:14), so that "where sin abounded, grace
abounded much more [exceedingly, ASV]" (Rom. 5:20).
Paul now lifts our hearts to give glory to God as "able
to do exceedingly abundantly above all that we ask or
think, according to the power that works in us"—nothing less than the exceeding greatness of the power that

raised Christ from the dead. And when we begin to see the possibility that God will work in us beyond all our imagination, He lifts our hearts to join in the universal chorus: "to Him be glory in the church by Christ Jesus to all generations, forever and ever. Amen" (Eph. 3:21).

As we worship and adore, we are called to believe in this almighty God who is working in our hearts according to His mighty power, able and willing to fulfill every one of His exceedingly great and precious promises and, where sin abounds, to prove that grace abounds more exceedingly.

Paul began his great prayer, "I bow my knees to the Father" (3:14). He ends it by bringing us to our knees, to give glory to Him as able to fulfill every promise, to reveal Christ as dwelling in our hearts, and to keep us in that life of love which leads to being filled with all the fullness of God.

Child of God, bow in deep adoration, giving glory to God, until your heart learns to believe that the prayer will be fulfilled. Jesus Christ will surely dwell in your heart by faith. Faith in this almighty God and in the exceeding abundance of His grace and power will teach us that the abiding indwelling of Christ in the heart is the secret of the abiding presence.

PUBLICATIONS

Fort Washington, PA 19034

This book is published by CLC Publications, an outreach of CLC
Ministries International. The purpose of CLC is to make evangelical
Christian literature available to all nations so that people may come
to faith and maturity in the Lord Jesus Christ. We hope this book has
been life changing and has enriched your walk with God through the
work of the Holy Spirit. If you would like to know more about CLC,
we invite you to visit our website:

www.clcusa.org

To know more about the remarkable story of the founding of
CLC International we encourage you to read

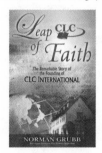

LEAP OF FAITH

Norman Grubb

Paperback
Size 5¹/₄ x 8, Pages 248
ISBN: 978-0-87508-650-7
ISBN (e-book): 978-1-61958-055-8

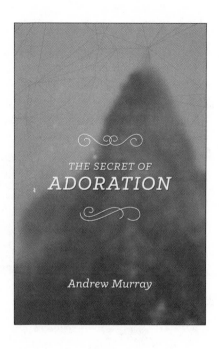

THE SECRET OF ADORATION

Andrew Murray

The Secret Series books contain a wealth of teaching that is based on Andrew Murray's mature and full experience in Christ. *The Secret of Adoration* contains one month of daily selections that highlight the importance of true worship in the lives of believers.

Paperback
Size 4¹/₄ x 7, Pages 71
ISBN: 978-1-61958-253-8
ISBN (*e-book*): 978-1-61958-254-5